Quiz Wizard

America
Past & Present
Trivia

Marsha Kranes, Fred Worth & Steve Tamerius
Edited by Michael Driscoll

THE
POPULAR
G R O U P

Popular Publishing Company, LLC
3 Park Avenue
New York, NY 10016

Cover art by Eileen Toohey

Cover and interior design by Tony Meisel

Manufactured in the United States of America

ISBN 1-59027-029-0

10 9 8 7 6 5 4 3 2 1

Questions

1. What room in the average American home is the scene of the greatest number of arguments?

2. How much does the 555-foot-5-$\frac{1}{8}$-inch-high Washington Monument in Washington, D.C., weigh?

3. What does Separation Creek in Oregon separate?

4. How many figures were tattooed on the body of Captain George Costentenus, one of the human curiosities put on exhibit by legendary showman P. T. Barnum in 1876?

5. In what year did motor vehicle registrations in the United States pass the million mark?

6. How many hours a year are Americans expected to spend waiting in traffic jams by the year 2005?

7. What is the length and width of the dollar bill?

8. Under California law, what fish may only be caught using bare hands?

Answers

1. The kitchen.

2. 90,854 tons.

3. Two mountains known as The Husband and The Wife.

4. From head to toe, 386—including fish, animals, birds, mummies and hieroglyphics.

5. In 1913, when there were 1,258,070 vehicles registered—1,190,393 of them passenger cars; 67,677 of them trucks and buses.

6. 8.1 billion, according to the Federal Highway Administration.

7. Length, 6.14 inches; width, 2.61 inches.

8. The tiny grunion, which comes ashore to spawn.

9. In 1960, the citizens of Hot Springs, New Mexico, voted to rename their town in honor of a popular radio show. What is it now called?

10. What are the names of the two landmark stone lions sitting in front of the New York Public Library at Fifth Avenue and 42nd Street in New York City?

11. How many windows are there on the 102-story Empire State Building?

12. How much time—in months—does the average American motorist spend during his lifetime waiting for red lights to turn green?

13. Borden is the name of a county in Texas. What is the name of its county seat?

14. Two states bill themselves as the "Sunshine State." Can you name them?

15. In 1954 the Pennsylvania coalmining communities of Maunch Chunk and East Maunch Chunk merged and adopted a new name in honor of a famous athlete. What was it?

16. What are school teams nicknamed at Jack Benny Junior High, the school the citizens of Waukegan, Illinois, named after their most famous son?

17. What was the name of the first series of U.S. postage stamps ever produced outside the country?

9. Truth or Consequences—*known as T or C for short. The change was made after radio (and later TV) show host Ralph Edwards promised to hold a program there annually.*

10. *Patience and Fortitude, names given them by Mayor Fiorello LaGuardia.*

11. *6,000.*

12. *Six months.*

13. *Gail, for Gail Borden, the man who brought us condensed milk—but only after drawing the first topographical map of Texas and surveying and laying out the city of Galveston.*

14. *Florida and South Dakota.*

15. *Jim Thorpe, after the great Oklahoma Indian athlete. The renaming was part of a plan to establish the town as a shrine to Thorpe, who was buried there.*

16. *The 39ers—39 was the age comedian Benny claimed for more than 39 years of his life.*

17. *Great Americans. The series, introduced in 1991, was printed in Canada.*

18. What employee-grooming regulation at Disney World would prevent the hiring of Walt Disney—if he were alive and job hunting today?

19. What was put between the steel framework and the copper skin of the restored Statue of Liberty to prevent corrosion?

20. On the reverse side of the $100 bill, what time is shown on the Independence Hall clock?

21. In what state can you find the towns of Romance, Sweet Home and Success?

22. Where are the only remaining free-roaming panthers in North America?

23. Why was the entire village of Hibbing, Minnesota, relocated?

24. What physical handicap afflicted Juliette Low, founder of the Girl Scouts of America?

25. Where did Samuel McPherson Hunt, gangster Al Capone's feared hitman, carry his submachine gun when he went out on a job?

26. In what unusual manner did Ashrita Furman retrace the 13 $\frac{1}{4}$-mile route taken by Paul Revere on his historic 1775 ride?

27. What U.S. city is at almost the same latitude as Mexico City?

18. The ban on facial hair. Disney had a mustache.

19. Teflon.

20. 4:10.

21. Arkansas.

22. In Southern Florida—in the Everglades and Big Cypress Swamp.

23. The village was sitting atop huge beds of iron ore. After it was moved south, the original site became one of the largest open-pit iron mines in the world—covering over 1,600 acres and running 535 feet deep.

24. She was deaf.

25. In a golf bag, rather than in the traditional violin case. His nickname was Golf Bag.

26. He somersaulted the entire way.

27. Hilo, on the Big Island of Hawaii. It's at 19˚42´ north; Mexico City is at 19˚ 25´ North.

28. In what state can you visit Athens, Carthage, Damascus, Egypt, England, Formosa, Hamburg, Havana, Holland, Jerusalem, London, Manila, Melbourne, Oxford, Palestine, Paris, Scotland and Stuttgart?

29. What was the first poll ever taken by national pulse-taker George Gallup?

30. What famous gangster, posing as a reporter for a detective magazine, convinced some cops to take him on a tour of the weapons arsenal in their police station—and later returned to steal everything in it?

31. What state is most dependent on tourism, with almost 30 percent of its jobs tourist related?

32. To whom was columnist Grantland Rice referring when he wrote: "Outlined against the blue-gray October sky, the Four Horsemen rode again"?

33. American naturalist George B. Grinnell founded the Audubon Society. What did his middle initial stand for?

34. Who gave his red hand-knitted cardigan sweater, size 38, to the Smithsonian Institution in 1984?

35. What's on the flip side of the Susan B. Anthony $1 coin?

36. How many Ringling Brothers were there?

28. Arkansas—which has towns with all of those names.

29. A survey to find the prettiest girl on campus at the University of Iowa, where he was editor of the student newspaper in the early 1920s. Gallup ended up marrying the winner, Ophelia Smith.

30. John Dillinger, in 1934. The police station was in Peru, Indiana.

31. The state of Nevada.

32. Notre Dame's undefeated 1924 backfield, Elmer Layden, Harry Stuhldreher, Don Miller, and Jim Crowley.

33. Bird.

34. Fred Rogers of public television's "Mister Rogers' Neighborhood."

35. An eagle landing on the moon, commemorating the Apollo II moon landing on July 20, 1969.

36. Seven: John, who headed the circus empire, and brothers Albert, Otto, Alfred, Charles, August, and Henry.

37. Which is the smallest of New York City's five boroughs—with a total area of 22.6 square miles?

38. What unique distinction does Maine's 5,268-foot Mt. Katahdin enjoy?

39. What is the only car that consumer crusader Ralph Nader has ever owned?

40. What oft-played American song's tune, meter, and verse form were borrowed from an English drinking song?

41. Mistletoe is the state flower of what state?

42. The names of 48 states are engraved on the frieze of the Lincoln Memorial, which was completed in 1922. How many are in the etching of the memorial on the back of the $5 bill?

43. What U.S. canyon is the deepest gorge on the North American continent?

44. What was the official New York City weather forecast on the day of the Great Blizzard of 1888?

45. What inland state has the longest shoreline?

46. What are the only four states to share a common boundary?

37. Manhattan. (Queens is the largest borough with 118.6 square miles.)

38. It is the first spot in the U.S. to be touched by the rays of the rising sun.

39. A 1949 Studebaker, which he sold thirty years ago when he was a Harvard Law School student.

40. "The Star Spangled Banner," which was based on the song "Anacreon in Heaven."

41. Rhode Island.

42. Twenty-six. Use a magnifying glass to check—they're in two rows on the frieze above the colonnade.

43. Hell's Canyon, also known as the Grand Canyon of the Snake River, which reaches a depth of 7,900 feet.

44. "Clearing and colder, preceded by light snow." The city was hit with 20.9 inches of snow and a temperature of - 6°F.

45. Michigan. Its more than 3,100 miles of freshwater shoreline includes four of the five Great Lakes—Michigan, Superior, Huron and Erie.

46. Arizona, Colorado, New Mexico, and Utah.

47. How did John Luther Jones, the engineer of the "Cannonball Express" whose death in a collision with a freight train is memorialized in ballad and legend, get his nickname "Casey"?

48. What three national parks does the Continental Divide pass through?

49. According to the folklore of the early American lumber camp, how was the Grand Canyon created?

50. How much does the Liberty Bell weigh?

51. What unearthly attraction can visitors find in Coconino National Forest, outside Flagstaff, Arizona?

52. How many islands are there in the Hawaiian Islands?

53. What is the origin of the name Baton Rouge, the capital of Louisiana?

54. What is the size of automobile license plates issued by the 50 states, Canada, and Mexico?

55. What is the name of the island on which Newport, Rhode Island, is located?

56. How long is the Grand Canyon of the Colorado River?

57. How did the town of Snowflake, Arizona, get its name?

47. *From his hometown: Cayce, Kentucky.*

48. *Yellowstone, Rocky Mountain and Glacier national parks.*

49. *By Paul Bunyan dragging his pick behind him.*

50. *Just over a ton—2,080 pounds.*

51. *A 640,000-square-foot re-creation of the lunar landscape blasted in the volcanic ash and cinders of a dry lake bed.*

52. *There are 132—8 major islands and 124 islets.*

53. *The name, translated from French, means "red stick"— for the red cypress tree that once marked the boundary between local Indian tribes.*

54. *They're 12 inches wide by 6 inches high.*

55. *Rhode Island—formerly Aquidneck. It gave its name to the state.*

56. *217 miles.*

57. *From two early settlers—Erastus Snow and William J. Flake.*

58. How much does it cost the U.S. government to produce a quarter?

59. How much does Plymouth Rock weigh?

60. What U.S. government agencies are known as Freddie Mac and Sallie Mae?

61. The Algonquin Hotel is a famous New York literary landmark. What is the name of the hotel down the street where the struggling young James Dean once lived?

62. How did Goon Dip Mountain, in Alaska, get its name?

63. What does verdigris have to do with the Statue of Liberty?

64. How many crayons does the average American child wear down in his or her coloring lifetime (ages 2 to 8)?

65. Where are the oldest church bells in the United States?

66. Where in the U.S. will you find both Neon and Krypton?

67. How did the town of Disco, Michigan, get its name?

58. 2 $\frac{1}{2}$ cents—which gives Uncle Sam a profit (or seigniorage) of 22 $\frac{1}{2}$ cents.

59. Approximately four tons.

60. Freddie is the Federal Home Loan Mortgage Corporation; Sallie, the Student Loan Marketing Association.

61. The Iroquois.

62. It was named in 1939 for Goon Dip, who had been the Chinese consul in Seattle.

63. It's the green patina on her copper body.

64. 730, according to the folks at Crayola.

65. In Boston's Old North Church. They were made in England in 1744 and shipped to Boston.

66. In Kentucky. They're small towns named after the two elements.

67. From a school once located there that was called Disco—which in Latin means "I learn."

68. What are the numbers of the three interstate highways that run from coast-to-coast?

69. How many elevators are there in the Empire State Building in New York City?

70. How many windows are there in the Pentagon, the world's largest office building?

71. What was the given name of Doc Holliday, the frontier dentist, gambler and gunman who befriended Wyatt Earp and was at his side during the shootout at the O.K. Corral?

72. Which American city was the first to establish a police department?

73. What comic strip character did the grateful farmers of Crystal City, Texas, honor with a six-foot-high stone mountain in 1937?

74. Who came in second to Eleanor Roosevelt in a 1945 *Fortune* magazine poll taken to determine the most famous woman in America?

75. Who once said: "The hardest thing in the world to understand is the income tax?"

76. Whose appearance in a nearly transparent white fishnet bathing suit in the 1978 *Sports Illustrated* swimsuit issue led an editor to promise, "We never have, and never will, run anything so revealing again"?

68. I-10, I-80 and I-90.

69. 73.

70. 7,754.

71. John Henry.

72. Boston. Regular-duty officers were appointed on May 5, 1838.

73. Popeye—for his role in popularizing spinach, their main crop.

74. The fictitious Betty Crocker, the symbol created in 1921 for General Mills' baking products.

75. Albert Einstein.

76. Cheryl Tiegs.

77. What was the average amount of money left per visit by the tooth fairy in 1950?

78. Why did Trinity College in Durham, North Carolina, change its name to Duke University in 1924?

79. How many official time zones are there in the United States—including Puerto Rico, the Virgin Islands and American Samoa?

80. Who owns the 45.52-carat Hope diamond?

81. What is the most frequently stolen street sign in New York City?

82. What was the total weight of the identical Dionne quintuplets—Annette, Cecile, Emilie, Marie and Yvonne—when they were born on May 28, 1934?

83. Prior to their complete 1998 redesign, how did $20 bills differ from those printed before 1948?

84. What name was originally spelled out in the huge mountainside sign that welcomes visitors in Hollywood?

85. Why is Arizona sometimes referred to as the Valentine State?

86. When you translate "revenue enhancement" from government doublespeak, what have you got?

77. *A quarter.*

78. *To honor its leading benefactor, tobacco tycoon James Buchanan Duke, and his family.*

79. *Eight. From Puerto Rico to Samoa, they are Atlantic, Eastern, Central, Mountain, Pacific, Alaska Standard, Hawaii–Aleutian and Samoa Standard.*

80. *The United States. It was given to the Smithsonian Institution by jeweler Harry Winston in 1958.*

81. *Hooker Place.*

82. *13 $\frac{1}{2}$ pounds.*

83. *The engraving of the White House on the back of the bill was changed in 1948 to include structural alterations made during Harry S. Truman's presidency. Additions include a balcony on the front portico and two more chimneys. Also different on the revised bill are the words below the engraving, which were changed from "White House" to "The White House."*

84. *Hollywoodland, the name of a real–estate subdivision on the site of what is now the nation's film capital.*

85. *It joined the Union as the 48th state on February 14, 1912.*

86. *A tax increase.*

87. What is the name of the tiny pond in New York's Adirondack Mountains where the 315-mile-long Hudson River originates?

88. What four state capitals are named after cities in England?

89. What was the name of pioneer Daniel Boone's family cat?

90. What words appear on the front of the penny, nickel, dime and quarter—alongside the likenesses of Presidents Lincoln, Jefferson, Franklin D. Roosevelt and Washington, respectively?

91. What is the name of the periodical published by the Procrastinators Club of America?

92. How deep is Oregon's Crater Lake, the deepest lake in the United States?

93. What car is shown in front of the U.S. Treasury Building on the back of the $10 bill?

94. How much garbage—in tons—is generated daily in the twin towers of the World Trade Center in New York City?

95. Which is the only state on the eastern seaboard to fall partially in the central time zone?

96. What city—more than 2 $\frac{1}{2}$ times the size of Rhode Island—is America's largest in area?

87. *Lake Tear of the Clouds.*

88. *Hartford, Connecticut; Dover, Delaware; Boston, Massachusetts; and Richmond, Virginia.*

89. *Bluegrass—which is also the nickname of Kentucky, the state he helped found.*

90. *"LIBERTY" and "IN GOD WE TRUST."*

91. *"Last Month's Newsletter"*

92. *1,932 feet deep. The lake is in the crater of Mount Mazama, an extinct volcano.*

93. *A 1926 Hupmobile.*

94. *65—of which about 37 $\frac{1}{2}$ tons are waste paper.*

95. *Florida.*

96. *Juneau, Alaska. It covers an area of 3,108 square miles. Rhode Island covers 1,214 square miles.*

97. Through how many states does U.S. 80—the main northern route from New York to California—pass?

98. Which two states have neighboring towns named for explorers Meriwether Lewis and William Clark?

99. Which of the 50 states takes in the least amount of tourist dollars?

100. What animals—besides horses—accompanied Buffalo Bill Cody when he sailed his Wild West Show to London in 1887 to appear before Queen Victoria?

101. What are roller coasters classified as by the U.S. Patent Office?

102. What is the name of the boulevard on which Fort Knox is located?

103. Which of the states uses the Napoleonic code rather than English common law as the basis of its civil law?

104. How many U.S. states and their capital cities have names that begin with the same letter?

105. What major vegetable crop was grown in Beverly Hills, California, before it became home to the rich and famous?

97. 12—*from east to west: New York, New Jersey, Pennsylvania, Ohio, Indiana, Illinois, Iowa, Nebraska, Wyoming, Utah, Nevada, California.*

98. *Idaho and Washington. The towns—Lewiston, Idaho, and Clarkston, Washington—are separated by the Snake River. Lewiston was a Lewis and Clark campsite.*

99. *Rhode Island. California takes in the greatest amount.*

100. *Buffalo (18), elk (10), mules (10), steers (5), donkeys (4) and deer (2). His cowboy–and–Indian entourage also included 180 horses.*

101. *Scenic railways. The classification was first used for roller coasters in 1886.*

102. *Bullion Boulevard.*

103. *Louisiana.*

104. *Four. Dover, Delaware; Indianapolis, Indiana; Oklahoma City, Oklahoma; and Honolulu, Hawaii.*

105. *Lima beans.*

106. What is the only place below sea level in the United States that is not in the California desert? Hint: It's a major city.

107. What aptly named village has the highest post office in the United States?

108. What newspaper, launched in 1982, was dubbed the McPaper because it provided its readers with "McNuggets" of news?

109. How fast—in words per minute—does the average American adult read?

110. How many steps are there to the top of the Empire State Building?

111. What is the best-selling magazine in the United States, and who founded it?

112. In 1949, Mrs. Ralph E. Smafield of Rockford, Ill., won first prize in what event with her Water-Rising Twists?

113. Who appeared on the cover of the maiden issue of *People* magazine on March 4, 1974?

114. What was Walt Disney's original title for his dream world, Disneyland?

115. Between 1835 and 1837 a now perennial feature of American life was blissfully absent. What was it?

106. New Orleans.

107. Climax, Colorado. It's located in the Rockies at 11,320 feet above sea level.

108. USA Today.

109. 275 words per minute.

110. 1,575.

111. "TV Guide," first published in 1953 by Walter Annenberg.

112. The first annual Pillsbury Bake-Off.

113. Mia Farrow.

114. Mickey Mouse Park.

115. The national debt.

116. Where is it illegal for a portrait of a living person to appear in the United States?

117. Who was *Time* magazine's Man of the Year for 1952?

118. In what connection is Anne Reese Jarvis remembered today?

119. Where is the longest street in the United States?

120. How was the three-mile territorial limit from the U.S. coastline determined?

121. What was the working title of Hugh Hefner's *Playboy* magazine, before it made its debut in December 1953?

122. What was the full name of the 8-year-old girl, Virginia, who wrote to the *New York Sun* asking if there really is a Santa Claus?

123. In what city did Will Rogers serve as honorary mayor?

124. Eighty-seven-year-old Democrat Rebecca Latimer Selton held what distinction in the political arena?

125. In 1992, the governor of Hawaii received a 30,000-signature petition to change the name of the island of Maui—to what?

116. On our postage stamps.

117. Queen Elizabeth II of Great Britain. It was her coronation year.

118. She was the inspiration for Mother's Day, which was dreamed up by her daughter, Anna M. Jarvis.

119. Los Angeles, where Figueroa Street runs for 30 miles.

120. It was the distance that coastal cannons could fire a shell.

121. "Stag Party."

122. Virginia O'Hanlon.

123. Beverly Hills.

124. She was the first woman to become a U.S. Senator, when she was appointed by the governor of Georgia to serve the remaining day of a vacated Senate seat, November 21–22, 1922.

125. Gilligan's Island, in honor of the TV sitcom. Needless to say, the island is still called Maui.

126. Which territory in North America did Detroit's founder, Antoine Laumet de la Mothe Cadillac, the man for whom the car is named, serve as governor from 1713 to 1716?

127. Whose body was the first to lie in state in the rotunda of the Capitol Building in Washington, D.C.?

128. What country benefited from the first foreign aid bill approved by the United States Congress?

129. What was the first building erected by the federal government in Washington, D.C.?

130. In a 1989 newspaper survey, only 9 percent of those polled knew William Rehnquist was chief justice of the U.S. Supreme Court. What judge was identified by 54 percent of those polled?

131. Of the 32 civil rights cases Thurgood Marshall argued before the U.S. Supreme Court as the lawyer for the National Association for the Advancement of Colored People, how many did he win?

132. Who was the first black American to win the Nobel Prize for Peace?

133. Which American colony was the first to enact anti-slavery legislation?

134. To what amount did Congress vote to raise the minimum wage on October 26, 1949?

126. Louisiana.

127. Senator Henry Clay's. He died in 1852.

128. Venezuela. In May 1812, Congress appropriated $50,000 for relief following an earthquake in Venezuela.

129. The executive mansion—later known as the White House. It was first occupied in 1800 by John Adams.

130. Retired California judge Joseph Wapner, of television's "The People's Court."

131. 29.

132. American statesman and United Nations official Ralph Bunche, in 1950, for his mediation of the 1948–49 Arab-Israeli War. Dr. Martin Luther King, Jr., whose birth we celebrate today, won the coveted award in 1964.

133. Massachusetts, in 1641, in its "Body of Liberties."

134. They raised it to 75 cents an hour; it had been 40 cents.

135. What did the U.S. government buy for Alaska's Eskimos in 1891?

136. What state was the last to adopt the secret ballot?

137. Uncle Sam made his first appearance—beardless—in 1852. When did he acquire whiskers?

138. What state abolished its personal income tax in 1980 and refunded $185 million already collected to its taxpayers?

139. What senator gave the longest filibuster on record—24 hours, 18 minutes?

140. How many years of schooling did Benjamin Franklin have?

141. John Jay, John Marshall, Roger B. Taney, and Salmon P. Chase were all chief justices of the U.S. Supreme Court. What other distinction did they share?

142. What was the name of the father of Sioux Indian leader Sitting Bull?

143. In 1812 New York City's Federal Hall—the site of America's first presidential inauguration—was torn down and sold for scrap at auction. How much did the city get for it?

135. Sixteen Siberian reindeer—the start of the state's herd.

136. South Carolina, in 1950.

137. In his seventeenth year, in 1869, in "Harper's Weekly" magazine.

138. Alaska, which has the highest per capita income in the country.

139. South Carolina Republican Strom Thurmond. He was opposing the 1957 voting rights bill.

140. Two—one year in grammar school and one with a private teacher.

141. They never went to law school.

142. Jumping Bull.

143. $425.

144. What was Martin Luther King, Jrs.'s name at birth?

145. Did Captain Miles Standish ever marry? You remember Standish, the Pilgrim leader who, according to legend, sought Priscilla Mullins' hand in marriage by having John Alden do the asking for him.

146. Who was the first civilian astronaut launched into space by the U.S.?

147. French daredevil aerialist Philippe Petit walked a tightrope linking the twin towers of New York's World Trade Center in 1974. How did he attach his 270-pound steel cable tightrope between the towers?

148. What is the significance of latitude 39°43' N in American history?

149. How long did America's first space flight, made by astronaut Alan Shepard, Jr., last?

150. Who wrote "Fish and visitors smell in three days"?

151. What was the name of the huge Newfoundland dog that accompanied explorers Meriwether Lewis and William Clark on their famous expedition to the Pacific northwest in the early nineteenth century?

152. What did Thomas Jefferson smuggle out of Italy in 1784 to help boost America's post-Revolution economy?

144. Michael Luther King Jr.

145. Standish married twice. Rose, his first wife, died during the Pilgrims' first winter in the New World. Barbara, whom he married in 1624, bore him six children. Standish was between wives when John supposedly spoke for himself and married Priscilla.

146. Neil Armstrong. The former Navy pilot went into space twice: in 1966 as commander of Gemini 8; in 1969 as commander of Apollo 11.

147. Friends used a bow and arrow to shoot a fishing line across the 131-foot gap—and then used the fishing line to pull the cable across.

148. It's the location of the Mason-Dixon Line, surveyed in the mid-eighteenth century to settle a boundary dispute between Pennsylvania and Maryland and considered the dividing line between North and South.

149. Shepard's suborbital flight in a 6-by-9-foot capsule lasted 15 minutes and 22 seconds.

150. Benjamin Franklin, in his wisdom-packed "Poor Richard's Almanack."

151. Scammon.

152. Jefferson snuck out two sacks of an improved strain of rice—despite a ban on its export from Italy—to help revitalize the Georgia and Carolina rice crops destroyed by the British during the Revolution.

153. How many states were created—in part or in their entirety—from the Louisiana Territory, purchased from France in 1803?

154. How many cherry trees had to be cut down to prepare the site for the Jefferson Memorial in Washington, D.C., in 1938?

155. Who gained fame as Richard Saunders during America's colonial days?

156. Who was the last man on the moon?

157. How many chests of tea were dumped overboard at the Boston Tea Party on December 16, 1773.

158. How long did the black boycott against the Montgomery, Alabama, bus system last?

159. What crime led to Billy the Kid's first run-in with the law?

160. When and where was the first recorded report of a UFO sighting made in the United States?

161. Which were the only four states to vote against the Sixteenth Amendment, the amendment ratified 80 years ago that gave Congress the power to "lay and collect taxes on incomes, from whatever sources derived"?

153. Thirteen: the entire states of Arkansas, Missouri, Iowa and Nebraska; and parts of Louisiana, Oklahoma, Kansas, Colorado, Wyoming, Montana, North Dakota, South Dakota and Minnesota.

154. 171.

155. Benjamin Franklin. Richard Saunders was the pen name he used in his "Poor Richard's Almanack" between 1732 and 1757.

156. Astronaut Eugene Cernan, commander of Apollo 17—in December 1972.

157. 342.

158. The boycott, led by the Rev. Martin Luther King, Jr., lasted 382 days. It ended when the city of Montgomery began integrated bus service on December 21, 1956.

159. The theft of some butter. His second known offense was receiving stolen property—clothes taken from a Chinese laundry.

160. In June 1947, near Mount Rainier, Washington. Idaho businessman Kenneth Arnold reported seeing nine silvery, saucer-shaped disks flying in formation at very high speed.

161. Connecticut, Florida, Rhode Island and Utah.

162. What article of clothing were women required to wear on the beach at New Jersey's Atlantic City until 1907—along with their standard attire of long bathing dresses, bathing shoes and straw hats?

163. How did Massachusetts sea captain Joshua Slocum—the first man to sail solo around the world—fight off pirates attacking his sloop?

164. What famous American's father headed the investigation into the Lindbergh kidnapping in 1932?

165. What triggered the legendary feud between the hillbilly Hatfields and McCoys in 1873?

166. What was the powder used by America's Founding Fathers to keep their wigs white?

167. Judge Roy Bean gained fame as the Law West of the Pecos. What was his brother, Josh, known for?

168. What was astronaut Neil Armstrong's total annual salary when he walked on the moon on July 20, 1969?

169. What was the name of the prospector who discovered gold in the Alaska panhandle in 1880?

170. In what year did the average American salary pass $100 a week?

171. Which state was the first in the nation to recognize Labor Day as a legal holiday?

162. Stockings.

163. He turned away the barefoot pirates by spreading carpet tacks on the deck of his boat. Slocum completed his historic 46,000-mile, 38-month voyage in 1898.

164. General H. Norman Schwarzkopf's. The senior Schwarzkopf was a retired brigadier general who was New Jersey's state chief of police at the time of the kidnapping.

165. The alleged theft of a pig.

166. Ground rice.

167. He was the first mayor of the city of San Diego, California.

168. Just over $30,000.

169. Joseph Juneau—the man for whom the capital of Alaska is named.

170. In 1963.

171. Oregon, in February 1887—followed later the same year by Colorado, Massachusetts, New Jersey and New York.

172. What famous Cherokee Indian was known to the Americans of his time as George Guess?

173. What famous words did Francis Bellamy write to commemorate the 400th anniversary of Columbus's discovery of America?

174. What was the name of the very first ocean-going vessel built by Englishmen in the New World?

175. What was the name of the first permanent settlement in Kentucky, established in 1775 by frontiersman Daniel Boone?

176. What role did the ships "Discovery," "Sarah Constant" and "Goodspeed" play in American history?

177. What house is the second-most-visited American home in the United States—outdrawn only by the White House?

178. In 1784 American settlers established an independent state named Franklin, in honor of Benjamin Franklin. Where was it?

179. How much expense money did Congress allot Meriwether Lewis and William Clark for their expedition across America that lasted from May 1804 to September 1806?

172. Sequoya.

173. "The Pledge of Allegiance"—which was published in "The Youth's Companion" magazine. Bellamy was on the magazine's staff.

174. Virginia. The 30-ton ship was built by settlers who landed in Maine in 1607, established a colony, but found life and the winter weather so harsh that they built a ship to escape a second winter.

175. Boonesborough.

176. They landed in what is now Jamestown, Virginia, in 1607, carrying the colonists who established the first permanent English settlement in the United States.

177. Graceland, the home of Elvis Presley in Memphis, Tennessee.

178. In what is now eastern Tennessee. The territory had been ceded to the federal government by North Carolina.

179. The sum of $2,500.

180. What famous frontierswoman was buried in Deadwood, South Dakota, wearing a white dress and holding a gun in each hand?

181. Who designed the Statue of Liberty's iron skeleton for French sculptor Frédéric Auguste Bartholdi?

182. What fashion was introduced by and named after Civil War Gen. Ambrose Burnside?

183. Why couldn't surgeon Charles Richard Drew, who organized the first blood bank in the U.S., donate his own blood?

184. What foreign government contributed the greatest amount of money for the relief of victims of the 1906 San Francisco earthquake?

185. What famous Northern publisher signed the bail bond for Confederate leader Jefferson Davis in 1867?

186. In 1867, how much per acre did the U.S. pay Russia for what is now the state of Alaska?

187. What movie had John Dillinger just seen when federal agents gunned him down outside the Biograph Theater in Chicago?

188. Who gave the "in" party for the Black Panthers that inspired the phrase "Radical Chic"?

180. Calamity Jane, aka Martha Jane Burke.

181. Alexandre Gustave Eiffel, who is best known for the tower that bears his name.

182. Sideburns—an anagram of his name.

183. Segregation laws in 1941 prohibited it—he was black.

184. Japan.

185. Horace Greeley, editor of the "New York Tribune."

186. Just under 2 cents, compared to 4 cents an acre paid for the Louisiana Territory in 1803.

187. "Manhattan Melodrama," in which "gangster" Clark Gable dies in the electric chair.

188. Conductor-composer Leonard Bernstein.

189. What American institution did Napoleon's grandnephew Charles Bonaparte found in 1908?

190. Who was the first U.S. citizen to be canonized as a saint?

191. Which state was the first to pass a right-to-die law?

192. The U.S. bought the Virgin Islands for $25 million in 1917—from what country?

193. What concession earned $862,000 in just five months at the Chicago World's Fair in 1933?

194. What was the Mayflower's cargo before it was chartered to carry the pilgrims to America in 1620?

195. What speed limit was set by Connecticut in 1901 in the first statewide automobile legislation passed in the U.S.?

196. What state was the first to proclaim Christmas a holiday?

197. What sentence did Patty Hearst receive in 1976 for the bank robbery she participated in while she was with the Symbionese Liberation Army?

198. What event was precipitated by a book entitled "Civic Biology"?

189. The F.B.I. He was attorney general of the U.S. at the time.

190. Mother Frances Xavier Cabrini, in 1946.

191. California, in 1976.

192. Denmark, which had established its first settlement there in 1672.

193. The rest room, at 5 cents a visit.

194. Wine. Just prior to its Atlantic crossing, the Mayflower transported 153 tuns and 16 hogsheads (39,564 gallons) of wine from Bordeaux to London.

195. On country highways, 15 mph; on highways within city limits, 12 mph.

196. Alabama, 150 years ago.

197. Seven years, but she served only 22 months—President Carter commuted her sentence.

198. The 1925 "Monkey Trial." "Civic Biology" was the text science teacher John Scopes read to his students in defiance of a Tennessee law banning the teaching of evolution.

199. What historical trial gave birth to the phrase "sharp as a Philadelphia lawyer"?

200. With what story did the tiny German-language newspaper "Philadelphische Staatshote" scoop the world?

201. What famous early American once boasted: "I can't say I was ever lost, but I was bewildered once for three days"?

202. How did the town of Showlow, Arizona, get its name?

203. From what European country did the ancestors of the people we call Pennsylvania Dutch originally come?

204. What were Robert E. Lee's dying words?

205. How many bullet holes did lawmen put in Clyde Barrow's car when they ambushed and killed him and his gangster girlfriend Bonnie Parker in 1934?

206. Which of the contiguous 48 states was the last to be explored?

207. What are the six flags that have flown over Texas?

199. The landmark 1735 libel trial of New York newspaperman John Peter Zenger, who was defended by Philadelphia lawyer Andrew Hamilton. Zenger was acquitted when the jury found his charges against the colonial governor were based on fact.

200. The adoption of the Declaration of Independence. The Staatshote (which, translated, means "Messenger of the State") was the only Philadelphia newspaper published on Fridays—and July 5th fell on a Friday in 1776.

201. Frontiersman Daniel Boone.

202. From the card draw held to pick the mayor of the mining town. The player who drew and showed the low card became mayor—giving the town its name. Its main street is called Deuce of Clubs in honor of the winning low card.

203. From Germany—the Dutch designation comes from the word Deutsch, meaning "German."

204. "Strike the tent."

205. They counted 106.

206. Idaho, which was first visited by Meriwether Lewis and William Clark in 1805 during their famous expedition across America.

207. The flags of Spain, France, Mexico, the Republic of Texas, the Confederacy, and the U.S.

208. Columbus had three ships on his first exploration of America. How many were under his command on his second expedition?

209. How did the American Indian brave shave?

210. How did the Pilgrims celebrate New Year's Day?

211. How many days did the historic civil rights march from Selma to Montgomery, Alabama, take?

212. According to poetic legend, Lizzie Borden used her ax to give her mother 40 whacks and her father 41. How many whacks did the police actually accuse her of delivering?

213. What does Apache chief Geronimo's Indian name—Goyathlay—mean in English?

214. How long did the April 18, 1906, earthquake in San Francisco last?

215. What were the dimensions of the "Star Spangled Banner" Francis Scott Key saw flying over Baltimore's Fort McHenry "by the dawn's early light" almost 185 years ago?

216. What size was the first footprint on the moon—the one made by astronaut Neil Armstrong when he took his historic "one small step for man" on July 20, 1969?

208. Seventeen.

209. With clam shells, which he used as tweezers.

210. They didn't. They considered it a blasphemous reverence for the Roman god Janus, for whom the month of January is named. The pilgrims referred to January as First Month.

211. Five days.

212. Dad, 10; stepmom, 19. But Lizzie was acquitted at her trial for the 1892 double slaying.

213. One who yawns. He was given the name Geronimo—Spanish for Jerome—by Mexicans.

214. 48 seconds. The San Francisco earthquake of 1989 lasted 15 seconds.

215. 30 feet by 42 feet. The fort's commander had it made that large so "the British will have no difficulty in seeing it from a distance."

216. It was 13 inches by 6 inches—the dimensions of Armstrong's boot. The exterior shell is the same size for all the astronauts' boots.

217. What were the police in Atlantic City, New Jersey, cracking down on when they arrested 42 men on the beach in 1935?

218. What is Mary E. Surratt's significance in U.S. history?

219. What did famed bank robber Charles Arthur "Pretty Boy" Floyd do whenever he pulled off a job, which made him a hero to many people?

220. How many children did Mormon leader Brigham Young have?

221. How many crates did it take to transport the Statue of Liberty from France to New York in 1885?

222. What did gangster Al Capone's oldest brother, Jim—who went by the name Richard "Two Gun" Hart—do for a living?

223. In an effort to avoid recapture, how did convicted bank robber Robert Alan Litchfield change his features after his 1989 escape from Fort Leavenworth, where he was serving a 140-year term?

224. Why didn't the anti-porn law passed by the town council of Winchester, Indiana, ever take effect?

225. What plant's leaves did American colonists use to brew a tea substitute following their Boston Tea Party tax protest?

217. *Topless swimsuits on men.*

218. *She was the first woman executed by hanging. A military panel convicted her of conspiracy in the assassination of President Abraham Lincoln. Her guilt, however, is still in question.*

219. *He destroyed all first mortgages he could find on the chance they had not been recorded, and tossed money out the window of his getaway car.*

220. *57, with 16 of his 27 wives.*

221. *214.*

222. *He was a lawman in Nebraska—serving as a town marshal and a state sheriff.*

223. *He underwent plastic surgery so he would look like actor Robert DeNiro.*

224. *The editors of the only newspaper in town refused to publish it, claiming the law itself was pornographic. Under local statutes, no law could take effect until published in a newspaper.*

225. *The goldenrod's—the drink it yielded was known as "liberty tea."*

226. When police and federal agents finally decoded the notation "K1,P2,CO8,K5" found in a Seattle woman's little black book in 1942, what did it turn out to be?

227. What was the name of the ship that was supposed to accompany the Mayflower on its historic journey across the Atlantic in 1620?

228. What well-known millionaire died when the Titanic sank?

229. What song was the band playing while the Titanic was sinking?

230. Who gave our country the name the United States of America?

231. Who was the only U.S. astronaut to fly in the Mercury, Gemini and Apollo programs?

232. What exactly did the Apollo II crew declare on a U.S. Customs form upon their return from the moon on July 24, 1969?

233. Who is infamous for staging the first train robbery?

234. What was the name of the ship on which Francis Scott Key composed "The Star Spangled Banner" in Baltimore Harbor, in 1814?

226. Knitting instructions: "Knit one, purl two, cast on eight, knit five."

227. The Speedwell. It was left behind in Plymouth, England, when it started taking on water.

228. John Jacob Astor.

229. Not "Nearer My God To Thee," as is popularly believed, but the hymn "Autumn," by Francois Barthelemon.

230. Thomas Paine.

231. Walter Shirra.

232. "Moon walk and moon dust samples."

233. Jesse James, at Adair, Iowa, on July 21, 1873.

234. The Minden.

235. French architect Pierre L'Enfant is best remembered in American history for what?

236. What was the name of the first child born of English parents in the New World?

237. John Glenn was the first American to orbit the earth. Who was the second?

238. How many women were among the first 105 colonists to settle in Jamestown, Virginia, in 1607?

239. When the first census of the United States was taken in 1790, what percentage of the population was African-American?

240. What was the name of the man who shot frontier legend Wild Bill Hickok in the back while he was playing poker in a Deadwood, South Dakota, saloon in 1876.

241. On what day of the week in 1492 did Christopher Columbus set sail for the New World?

242. What was originally on the site of America's first mint, the Philadelphia mint, which opened in 1792?

243. What bird was imported to the United States from England in 1850 to protect shade trees from voracious, foliage-eating caterpillars?

244. What were the five tribes in the Iroquois League when it was formed around 1600?

235. He planned the city of Washington, D.C. in 1791. It was known at the time as Federal City.

236. Virginia Dare, who was born in 1587 on Roanoke Island.

237. Scott Carpenter, on May 24, 1962.

238. None. The first two women settlers arrived in 1609.

239. 19.3 percent—of which 59,557 were free blacks and 697,624 were slaves.

240. Jack McCall. He was acquitted at a trial the day after the shooting, then retried and hanged.

241. Friday.

242. A distillery.

243. The English (or house) sparrow. Eight pairs were imported by the Brooklyn Institute in New York. They multiplied so prolifically that in 1890, New York City imported starlings to prey on the sparrows in Central Park.

244. The Mohawk, Seneca, Onondaga, Oneida and Cayuga. The league later expanded to six tribes when it admitted the Tuscarora.

245. How many stripes were on the official American flag in 1818 before Congress passed a law forever setting the number at 13?

246. How many signatures are on the Declaration of Independence?

247. How was Martha's Vineyard spelled on official U.S. government maps before 1933?

248. Who was the first European explorer to see and cross the Mississippi River?

249. What famous Old West town was known as Goose Flats before a prospector named Ed Schieffelin discovered silver there?

250. How much did the multi-layered space suits worn by astronauts on the Apollo moon landings weigh—life-support system included?

251. What city was the center of gold mining in the United States before the discovery of gold at Sutter's Mill in 1848 triggered the California gold rush?

252. How many children did Pocahontas and her husband John Rolfe have?

253. A likeness of what famous legendary figure was on the prow of the first ship to bring Dutch settlers to America?

245. 15. The number had been increased to 15 in 1795 to include Kentucky and Vermont. But with more and more states joining the Union, the number was reduced to 13 as of July 4, 1818, to represent the original 13 states.

246. 56.

247. Marthas Vineyard. The apostrophe making the name possessive was the first apostrophe sanctioned by the U.S. Board on Geographic Names.

248. Hernando de Soto of Spain, in 1541. He died the following year.

249. Tombstone, Arizona. Schieffelin picked the name because soldiers laughingly told him all he'd find there would be his tombstone when he set out to prospect in the area in the 1870s.

250. On earth, 180 pounds; on the moon, with the reduced lunar gravity, 30 pounds.

251. Charlotte, North Carolina. From 1800 to 1848, gold mines in the Charlotte area were the main source of U.S. gold.

252. One, a son named Thomas, who was born and educated in England but settled in Virginia.

253. Sinterklass—a predecessor of Saint Nicholas, better known to us as Santa Claus.

254. How many states were there in the United States at the turn of the century?

255. What is the diameter of each of the two main cables on San Francisco's Golden Gate Bridge?

256. For what famous historic figure was Marietta, Ohio, named?

257. What role did the ships Dartmouth, Beaver and Eleanor play in American history?

258. Which American state capital was originally incorporated as the town of Marthasville?

259. What famous Englishman gave us the expression, "Keep your powder dry"?

260. How long—in days—did the Pilgrims' first Thanksgiving in 1621 last?

261. How much was suffragette Susan B. Anthony fined for voting in 1872?

254. 45. Oklahoma became the 46th state in 1907; followed by New Mexico and Arizona in 1912; and Alaska and Hawaii in 1959.

255. 3 feet—or 36.5 inches, to be exact. There are 25,572 wires contained in each of the cables.

256. Marie Antoinette.

257. They were the three ships targeted by American colonists at the Boston Tea Party on December 16, 1773. Together the three ships had 342 casks of the tea dumped into Boston Harbor by colonists who disguised themselves as Mohawks to carry out their historic protest of the British tax on tea.

258. Atlanta, Georgia, in 1843—in honor of Martha Lumpkin, daughter of the governor of the state. A railroad official changed the name two years later to Atlanta, the feminine of Atlantic, after the Western and Atlantic Railroad, which had selected the town as the last stop on its line.

259. Oliver Cromwell. In 1642 at the Battle of Edgehill, he told his troops, "Put your trust in God, but keep your powder dry."

260. Three. It featured bountiful meals, demonstrations by the Plymouth militia, traditional Indian dancing by the native guests, and foot races and other athletic contests.

261. $100.

262. What was the source of E pluribus unum—Latin for "one from many"—the motto the Second Continental Congress adopted for the Great Seal of the newly named United States?

263. How many times does each newly produced U.S. dollar bill have to go through the printing press?

264. According to the Census Bureau, what are the five most common surnames in the United States?

265. Where were the Library of Congress's original copies of the U.S. Constitution and the Declaration of Independence kept during World War II?

266. Which state is America's flattest, with a difference of only 345 feet between its highest and lowest points?

267. Which state is the most thickly forested, with 89.8 percent of its land area classified as wooded by the U.S. Forest Service?

268. How many jurors were dismissed during the course of O. J. Simpson's double-murder trial?

269. How many ballots in the House of Representatives did it take to break the deadlocked presidential election between Thomas Jefferson and Aaron Burr in February 1801?

270. How fast—in miles per hour—do the fastest roller coasters in the U.S. go?

262. It was from a recipe for salad in a poem entitled "Moretum," attributed to Virgil. The words, chosen by Benjamin Franklin, John Adams and Thomas Jefferson, were known at the time because they appeared as a motto on the cover of Gentlemen's Magazine.

263. Three. First the front is printed in black, then the back is printed in green, and finally, the front is over-printed with the serial number and Treasury Department seal in green.

264. Smith, Johnson, Williams, Jones and Brown, in that order.

265. At Fort Knox, Kentucky

266. Florida. Delaware is the second flattest state, with an elevation range of 442 feet.

267. Maine. It's followed by New Hampshire, at 88.1 percent, and West Virginia, with 77.5 percent.

268. 10.

269. 36.

270. The two fastest—the Steel Phantom in West Mifflin, Pennsylvania, and the Desperado in Jean, Nevada—reach a speed of 82 miles an hour.

271. How many signers of the Declaration of Independence went on to serve as president of the United States?

272. What was the country of origin of the greatest number of immigrants to pass through Ellis Island between 1892 and 1924?

273. How many states border an ocean?

274. Where is the Superman Museum located?

275. What words did Thomas Jefferson use in his final draft of the Declaration of Independence to describe the truths we now hold to be "self-evident"?

276. What interest rate was charged when the U.S. government took out its first loan in September 1789 to help pay the salaries of the president and Congress?

277. How much—in pounds and shillings—did Paul Revere charge in expenses for his ride to New York and Philadelphia to deliver news of the Boston Tea Party in December 1773?

278. What motto was inscribed on the 1787 Fugio cent, the first coin issued by authority of the United States?

271. Two—John Adams and Thomas Jefferson.

272. Italy, with 2.5 million. It was followed by Austria-Hungary, 2.2 million; Russia, 1.9 million; and Germany, 633,000.

273. 23. They are: Maine, New Hampshire, Massachusetts, Rhode Island, Connecticut, New York, New Jersey, Delaware, Maryland, Virginia, North Carolina, South Carolina, Georgia, Florida, Alabama, Mississippi, Louisiana, Texas, California, Oregon, Washington, Alaska and Hawaii.

274. In Metropolis, Illinois. The comic book superhero lived and worked as Clark Kent in a fictional city named Metropolis.

275. Jefferson wrote "sacred and undeniable," but Benjamin Franklin, acting as his editor, changed the wording to "self-evident." In all, 86 changes were made to the draft submitted by Jefferson.

276. Six percent. The loan, for $200,000, was from the Bank of New York. A similar loan was obtained from the Bank of North America.

277. 14 pounds, 2 shillings. The trip took him 11 days. His bill, endorsed by John Hancock, was sold at auction in 1978 for $70,000.

278. "Mind your business." The motto was suggested by Benjamin Franklin. Fugio is Latin for "I am fleeing"—meaning time flies.

279. After what famous eatery did railroad innovator George Pullman name his first luxury dining car in 1832?

280. How many male justices had been appointed to the U.S. Supreme Court before Sandra Day O'Connor became the first woman named to the nation's highest court?

281. What are the eight Rocky Mountain states?

282. How long did it take aerialist Philippe Petit to make his 1,350-foot-long tightrope walk between the twin towers of the World Trade Center in New York City in 1974?

283. What state capital was originally called Pig's Eye?

284. What famous Indian chief's name was Goyakla or Goyathlay, which means One Who Yawns in his native tongue?

285. In the early years of America's celebration of Mother's Day, what flower was customarily worn by those honoring their moms?

286. What did "Little Miss Sure Shot" Annie Oakley do with all her gold shooting medals?

287. What percent of a newly minted dime is silver?

279. Delmonico's, the fashionable New York restaurant.

280. 104. She was nominated to the Supreme Court in 1981 by Ronald Reagan.

281. Idaho, Montana, Wyoming, Nevada, Utah, Colorado, Arizona and New Mexico.

282. 50 minutes.

283. St. Paul, Minnesota. Pig's Eye was the nickname of one of the town's first settlers, a French–Canadian trader named Pierre Parrant.

284. The Apache we know as Geronimo, Spanish for Jerome.

285. The carnation. Pink carnations were worn by those whose mothers were alive; white by those whose mothers had died.

286. She had them melted down, then sold the gold and gave the money to charity.

287. None. As of 1965, the U.S. Mint stopped putting silver in dimes. They contain 75 percent copper and 25 percent nickel, bonded to an inner core of pure copper. Previously, dimes were 90 percent silver and 10 percent copper.

288. For what is the telephone number 800-555-0199 reserved?

289. What three names were given to more than half the females christened in the Massachusetts Bay Colony in the 1600s?

290. What group of Americans speak a dialect they call Mudderschprooch?

291. What shipboard position did John Washington, George Washington's grandfather, hold when he sailed from England to Virginia aboard the ketch Sea Horse of London in 1657?

292. What Ivy League college was the last to go coed?

293. What Old West city was named after a biblical city that drew its name from the Hebrew word for "grassy plain."

294. How many U.S. states are there with only four letters in their names? Watch out, this is a trick question.

295. What American city claims to have the only authentic Dutch windmill in the country?

296. How long must a person be dead before he or she can be honored with a U.S. commemorative stamp?

288. The movies. It's the 800 number set aside for use in films.

289. Sarah, Elizabeth and Mary.

290. The Amish. The language is Pennsylvania Dutch.

291. He was a ship's mate. Although Washington intended to return to England with the ketch and a cargo of tobacco, the ship sank and he stayed in the colonies.

292. Dartmouth, in 1972.

293. Abilene, Kansas, which was entirely grassland when it was named in the mid-nineteenth century and served as the end of the famous Chisholm Trail. The biblical Abilene (from the Hebrew word abel) is mentioned in Luke 3:1 and was in ancient Syria.

294. Nine. The easy ones are Iowa and Utah. The tough ones are Alabama, Alaska, Hawaii, Indiana, Kansas, Mississippi and Tennessee.

295. Aptly named Holland, Michigan, founded in 1847 by Dutch immigrants and site of an annual tulip festival. The city's centuries-old windmill was dismantled in Vinkel, Holland, and reassembled there in 1965.

296. At least 10 years—except for U.S. presidents. Commemorative stamps can be issued for a deceased president on the first birthday anniversary following his death, or anytime thereafter.

297. In airport code, LAX stands for Los Angeles International Airport and JFK for Kennedy International Airport. What airport is represented by the initials IAD?

298. What weekly periodical was the first magazine in history to sell a billion copies in a year?

299. What was the dark blue Crayola crayon called before its name was changed to midnight blue in 1958?

300. What did Wild Bill Hickok toss around his bed so he wouldn't be surprised by anyone sneaking up on him while he slept?

301. What state has an average of 124 tornadoes a year—more than any other?

302. What name was given to the largest diamond ever found in the U.S.?

303. What did the middle initial O stand for in the late Supreme Court Justice William O. Douglas's name?

304. What number iron did astronaut Alan Shepard use when he took his famous swing at a golf ball on the moon?

305. What is the flickertail, from which North Dakota gets its official state nickname, the Flickertail State?

297. *Dulles International Airport in Washington, D.C.*

298. *"TV Guide," in 1974.*

299. *Prussian blue. It was the first crayon renamed by Binney & Smith, which started producing crayons in 1903.*

300. *Crumpled newspapers.*

301. *Texas. In second place is Oklahoma, which averages 56 tornadoes a year.*

302. *The Uncle Sam diamond. It was 40.23 carats in the rough when it was found in Murfreesboro, Arkansas, in 1924, and it yielded a 12.42-carat gem.*

303. *Orville.*

304. *A six. The club actually was a 6-iron head attached to a jointed astronaut tool used to scoop soil.*

305. *A squirrel—the Richardson ground squirrel—widely found in North Dakota.*

306. What did Robert LeRoy Ripley, creator of the Believe It or Not newspaper cartoons, call his oddity-filled 27-room home?

307. How many of the ships involved in Columbus's historic 1492 expedition made return voyages to the New World?

308. American dollar bills are not printed on paper as many believe—what are they printed on?

309. What famous American statesman made three appearances on national TV as a weather forecaster?

310. According to Senate tradition, who is assigned the desk once occupied by Daniel Webster?

311. What famous Old West lawman was appointed deputy U.S. marshal for New York by Theodore Roosevelt?

312. What state's official bird is the roadrunner?

313. How many terms did American frontiersman Davy Crockett serve in Congress?

314. What figure in American history is believed to have inspired the exclamation "Great Scott"?

315. How fast was New York City cabbie Jacob German driving when he became the first motorist arrested in the U.S. for speeding?

306. Bion—for Believe It or Not.

307. Only one—the Niña. The Santa Maria, Columbus's flagship, ran aground off Hispaniola and was abandoned on the first expedition; the Pinta sailed home from the New World and disappeared from history.

308. Fabric—a cotton linen blend.

309. Former secretary of state and national security advisor Henry Kissinger, in 1991.

310. The senior senator from New Hampshire. The tradition was established by New Hampshire Senator Styles Bridges, who discovered the desk in the basement of the Capitol. (Webster, who represented Massachusetts in the Senate, was born in New Hampshire.)

311. Bat Masterson.

312. New Mexico's.

313. Three.

314. Gen. Winfield Scott—the hero of the Mexican War and the losing candidate for president in 1852.

315. 12 miles an hour. The year was 1899, and the arresting officer was on a bicycle.

316. What was the first word spoken on the moon?

317. What was Benjamin Franklin explaining when he said, "An ounce of prevention is worth a pound of cure"?

318. How many banks and trains did the notorious Jesse James rob?

319. What was the name of De Tour Village, Michigan, before it was changed?

320. What was the first country to which the United States sent a woman as ambassador?

321. Of the 14 states bordering on the Atlantic, which has the least oceanfront—only 13 miles?

322. What did the town of Ismay, Montana, change its name to in 1993?

323. How did Embarrass, Wisconsin, get its name?

324. What was the weekly salary paid to Chief Sitting Bull when he was part of Buffalo Bill Cody's traveling Wild West Show?

325. What is the only crime defined in the U.S. Constitution?

326. When the first U.S. Congress set the president's pay at $25,000 a year, what salary did it establish for the vice president?

316. "Houston." Astronaut Neil Armstrong's first message on July 20, 1969, was: "Houston, Tranquillity Base here. The Eagle has landed."

317. Why he had just attached a lightning rod to his house.

318. Banks, 12; trains, 7.

319. Detour. It was changed to avoid confusion with road signs. The village is located on Lake Huron at the eastern tip of Michigan's Upper Peninsula.

320. Denmark, in 1933. Ruth Bryan Owen, a two-term congresswoman and the daughter of William Jennings Bryan, served until 1936 when she married Danish citizen Borge Rohde.

321. New Hampshire. Florida has the most, 580 miles.

322. Joe, Montana, in honor of the star quarterback.

323. The village's founding fathers weren't commemorating an event that left them red-faced. They took the name from a local river that lumberjacks often found impassable—and embarras is French for "hindrance" or "obstacle."

324. $50.

325. Treason—in Article III, Section 3.

326. $5,000.

327. In what state was the Battle of Tippecanoe fought in November 1811?

328. El Paso is known as the Four C City. What attractions do the four C's represent?

329. Under the rules of the Senate Ethics Committee, what is the maximum number of times a senator's name can appear in a newsletter to his or her constituents?

330. Who represented Aaron Burr's wife, Eliza Jumel, when she sued her 80-year-old husband for divorce on grounds of adultery in 1836?

331. What was the name of Paul Bunyan's pet moosehound?

332. What state has official neckwear?

333. In what year did the F. B. I, established in 1908 as the Bureau of Investigation, start hiring women as special agents?

334. The flag of what American state was designed by a 13-year-old- boy?

335. At what constant speed does the cable that pulls San Francisco's famous cable cars move—in miles per hour?

336. Who was the first African-American to have his portrait engraved on a U.S. coin?

327. Indiana.

328. Cattle, climate, copper and cotton.

329. An average of eight times per page. The rule applies to franked (postage-exempt) mail.

330. Alexander Hamilton, Jr., son of the man Burr killed in his famous duel. Jumel was granted a legal divorce on the day of Burr's death.

331. Elmer.

332. Arizona—the bolo tie.

333. In 1972—after the death of longtime director J. Edgar Hoover, who had banned women agents.

334. Alaska. Seventh-grader Benny Benson entered the design—of the Big Dipper and the North Star on a field of blue—in an American Legion contest in 1927. It was adopted as the territorial flag, and later as the state flag.

335. 9 mph.

336. Booker T. Washington, on a commemorative silver half-dollar issued from 1946 to 1951.

337. What was the late Supreme Court Justice Thurgood Marshall's first name at birth?

338. What was the featured attraction between the Indian elephant act and the ape-man act at the Barnum & Bailey Circus in 1896?

339. Where was Billy the Kid, the notorious Wild West outlaw, born?

340. In what city did the high-kicking Rockettes of New York's Radio City Music Hall get their start?

341. How has American veterinarian and U.S. Agriculture Department inspector Daniel E. Salmon (1850-1914) been immortalized?

342. What was the last institution of higher learning in the United States established by royal decree?

343. What mountain has the most extensive glacial system of any single peak in the contiguous 48 states?

344. What was the Declaration of Sentiments, drafted in Seneca Falls, New York, in 1848?

345. What was the name of strongman-bodybuilder Charles Atlas's son?

337. Thoroughgood—he shortened it when he was in the second grade.

338. An automobile. American auto pioneer Charles Duryea drove around in one of the 13 autos his Duryea Motor Wagon Company produced that year.

339. In New York City, as Henry McCarty, in 1859. He later changed his name to Henry Antrim, then to William (Billy the Kid) Bonney.

340. In St. Louis. The dancing group was organized there in 1925 as the Missouri Rockets. After changing the name to the Roxyettes, the group moved to Radio City, becoming the Rockettes in 1932.

341. Salmonella—the sometimes deadly bacteria—is named for him.

342. Dartmouth College, which received its royal charter from England's King George III in 1769.

343. Mount Rainier, in Washington State. It has a total of 26 named glaciers.

344. A treatise, patterned after the Declaration of Independence, that declared "All men and women are created equal." It was signed by 100 people—68 women and 32 men—at the nation's first women's rights convention.

345. Hercules. He grew up to become a math teacher.

346. What was Benjamin Franklin's last official act?

347. What body of water did the early American settlers describe as "too thick to drink, too thin to plow"?

348. What is the name of the 600-mile-long California trail that the Spanish blazed from mission to mission from San Diego to Sonoma?

349. What role did Garret A. Hobart play in American history?

350. In what city was the first stock exchange in the United States established?

351. Who wrote the unofficial anthem of Hawaii, "Aloha Oe"?

352. What famous early Americans named North America's whistling swan?

353. How many single-serving jars of baby food does the average American baby eat in one year?

354. In 1910 there were 32 million Americans living on farms. How many were living on farms in 1990?

355. How was a man named Fred Ott immortalized by Thomas Edison?

346. Two months before his death in 1790, he signed a petition to Congress calling for the abolition of slavery. He did so as president of the Pennsylvania Society for Promoting the Abolition of Slavery.

347. The Mississippi River, which is nicknamed the Big Muddy.

348. El Camino Real. It linked 21 missions and 4 forts.

349. Vice president (1897–99) to William McKinley—Hobart died while in office.

350. In Philadelphia, in 1790—two years before a New York exchange was set up.

351. Queen Liliuokalani—the last royal ruler of the Hawaiian Islands.

352. Explorers Meriwether Lewis and William Clark, who discovered the swan and named it for its song during their expedition to the West Coast.

353. 630, according to the folks at Gerber Products.

354. 4.6 million.

355. Edison filmed him sneezing in the first copyrighted film in history.

356. What late Nobel Peace Prize-winning world leader was once a wanted terrorist with a $50,000 bounty on his head?

357. How did Charles Lindbergh's Spirit of St. Louis get back to the U.S. after its historic 1927 transatlantic flight to Paris?

358. Where was the flower known as the Yellow Rose of Texas first found in the United States?

359. How wide are the stars from point to point on the flag
that inspired Francis Scott Key to write "The Star-Spangled Banner"?

360. What two changes have been made in the wording of the U.S. Pledge of Allegiance since it was first published in 1892?

361. How many birthday cards does the average person receive annually?

362. What magazine regularly publishes a column called "Streetwalker"?

363. The name of what American state capital means "sheltered harbor."

356. Israeli Prime Minister Menachem Begin. The bounty was offered by British authorities in 1946 when Begin led the Irgun underground guerrillas in their fight for Zionist homeland. He shared the Nobel Prize with Egyptian President Anwar Sadat in 1978.

357. In a pine packing crate, measuring 27 by 12 by 9 feet, that was put aboard the cruiser USS Memphis.

358. In New York City. A lawyer named George Harrison found it as a seedling in the 1830s on his farm near what is now Penn Station. The rose was brought out west by settlers and—according to legend—adopted by Texans after Mexican General Santa Anna was distracted by a beautiful woman wearing it in her hair.

359. Two feet across. The flag is now on display at the Smithsonian Institute in Washington, D.C.

360. The words "the flag of the United States of America" replaced the original words "my flag" in 1923; and the phrase "under God" was added in 1954.

361. Eight, according to the folks at Hallmark.

362. Forbes. The street referred to, of course, is Wall Street.

363. Honolulu.